Melinda Marie Moore-Johnson

Aunt Mittie

Goes to Church

ii

Copyright © 2019 by Melinda Marie Moore Johnson

All rights reserved. No part of this publication may be reproduced, distributed, or transmitted in any form or by any means, including photocopying, recording, or other electronic or mechanical methods, without the prior written permission of the publisher, except in the case of brief quotations embodied in critical reviews and certain other noncommercial uses permitted by copyright law.

ISBN: 978-1-7336754-9-9

Liberation's Publishing LLC
West Point, Mississippi
www.liberationspublishing.com

This book is dedicated to

The Holy Spirit

My Family

Clarence Allen Johnson

Jesse & Shalisha Lakisha Owens

Tasheera Brenade Johnson & Keith Fields

Greg Green & Auriel Latrese Green

Jermale & Marnita McCarter

J.P. Duck Jr. & Contrina Duck

All my Grandchildren

Vera Smith-Moore (Deceased) & Jessie (Joe) Moore (Deceased)

Susie Nichol (Deceased)

Brothers & Sisters

Brother-in-laws & Sister-in-laws

Nephews & Nieces

Pastor Charlie Frank Barnes, Sr. & Sis. Dovie Barnes

Mount Peiler MB Church Family Friends

Emma Gibson-Gandy & Calvin Ware

To my husband Clarence Allen Johnson for his words of encouragement and his unconditional love he has for me. A special feeling of gratitude to Ms. Susie Nichols is deceased but I thank her and her family for making Aunt Mittie a part of my life.

And the love that my children and grandchildren shown me why preparing this book.

Aunt Mittie always walked to church with her big sister. She loved going to church and loved Sunday school even more. Aunt Mittie would sing all the way to Sunday school. Today was no different,

"It's me, it's me, it's me oh Lord. Standing in the need of prayer" she sang swing her little white purse. She continued singing and walking. She was so excited.

People driving past would wave and smile. It was Sunday so no one was in a hurry. "Hi," Aunt Mittie paused from singing and waved. After a while, Tick Tock Baptist Church was in view.

"Come on Sis," Aunt Mitties shouts, "Let's get inside before we miss something." Aunt Mittie's sister smiles and takes her hand.

Tick Tock Baptist Church was a family church. Many of Aunt Mittie's aunts, uncles, and cousins attended. Inside Aunt Mittie had a regular seat. She sat there quietly until Sunday School started. No playing in God's house for Aunt Mittie. She respected God's things very much. She had a special gift on her life and loved just being in God's house.

Deacon By was one of the oldest deacons Tick Tock Baptist Church had. Deacon By calls the service to order. He stood up front and asked all the visitors to stand.

"Good morning members and friend," Deacon By says. "Do we have anyone visiting us today?"

A few visitors stood up. "We welcome you to Tick Tock Baptist Church. Here at Tick Tock Baptist Church everybody is somebody, and we are all GOD children." Deacon By says with great joy, "Praise GOD! Praise GOD! Sunday school is now in progress! Sunday school is now in progress!" He liked repeating things too.

Tick Tock Baptist Church

Usually the adult did the devotion. Today was Aunt Mittie's lucky day. She raised her hand and waved it quickly back and forth, all the while not saying a word. Jack her cousin waved his hand also.

"Praise God," shouts Deacon By, "I have two volunteers.

Aunt Mittie and Jack walked to the front fast and excited.

Deacon By replied, "Aunt Mittie what will you sing for us today?"

"I will sing "It's me, it's me, it's me, Oh LORD standing in the need of prayer".

"Aunt Mittie that is a wonderful idea! That is my favorite song," Deacon By replied.

Aunt Mittie starts to sing and everyone else joined in. She closed her eyes and start singing from her heart like a humming bird. She had a beautiful voice.

After Aunt Mittie finished singing, Jack read the scripture. After Jack finished reading the scripture, Deacon By got up to take over the Sunday school service.

"Praise God," he said, "thank you children, thank you children. Job well done. Thank you for letting the Lord use you. Church the LORD is in this place, because that song and scripture was in my spirit this morning. Job well done children! Job well done!"

After devotion everyone scattered to their Sunday school class. Aunt Mittie always got at the end of the line to her class. She was responsible for picking up the roll book. She kept smiling and humming to herself. When her class walked by the clerk's office, she picked up the roll book.

Sister Lakisha the church's clerk heard Aunt Mittie singing, "who is that singing my favorite song?" she asked.

"It's me, Sister Lakisha," Aunt Mittie replied, "good morning."

Sister Lakisha handed Aunt Mittie the roll book for her class. "Here you go Aunt Mittie."

"Thank you, sister Have a wonderful day," Aunt Mittie said proud and happy.

"Aunt Mittie you are so blessed. I can tell you love the Lord."

Sister Brenade the assistant clerk comes out of the back and joins the conversation. "Yes, you can,"

Sister Brenade said, "And she loves working in the church."

"She is a good role model," said Sister Lakisha.

"Yes, God is using her to show others how to share his love," Sister Brenade replied.

"God is love," said Aunt Mittie, "All is well Lord, all is well."

www.ingramcontent.com/pod-product-compliance
Lightning Source LLC
Chambersburg PA
CBHW061146070526
44584CB00033B/4441